To Help Is Profit

How to Make a Profit By Impacting the Lives of Others

THE EXCEPTIONAL

Copyright © by The Exceptional 2023. All rights reserved.

Before this document is duplicated or reproduced in any manner, the publisher's consent must be gained. Therefore, the contents within can neither be stored electronically, transferred, nor kept in a database. Neither in Part nor full can the document be copied, scanned, faxed, or retained without approval from the publisher or creator.

Table of Contents

I. Introduction

II. Benefits of Helping Others

III. The Value of Compassion

IV. 10 Ways to Help Others and Make a Difference in Their Lives

V. 10 Ways to Make a Profit by Helping Other People

VI. How Facebook Makes Money by helping businesse

VII. Conclusion

Introduction

Helping others is an important part of life. It is something that everyone should do in order to make the world a better place. Helping others can give us a sense of purpose and fulfillment, and can even improve our own mental and physical health. When we help others, we can learn more about ourselves, build relationships, and create a stronger sense of community. Helping others can create a ripple effect of positive change in our society, and can help create a more positive and inclusive environment for everyone.

When we help others, we are not only making a difference in their lives, but also in our own. Studies show that helping others can reduce stress, improve self-confidence, and even boost our immune systems. Helping others can also give us a sense of purpose and satisfaction that can improve our overall happiness. In addition to these mental and physical benefits, helping others can also help build stronger relationships and create a stronger sense of community.

No matter how small the act of kindness may be, it can make a big difference in the lives of others. Whether it's volunteering at a local charity, donating to a cause, or simply lending a helping hand to a friend in need, helping others can have an immense impact on our lives. So, let's all make an effort to help others and make the world a better place.

Helping others is important for a variety of reasons. It not only has a positive effect on the people we help, but it also has a positive effect on ourselves. Helping others can make us feel good about ourselves, reduce our stress and boost our emotional health. It can also help us build relationships and connect with those around us. In addition, helping others can open up new opportunities and help us develop new skills. Ultimately, helping others is a great way to feel fulfilled and make a positive impact on the world

Chapter 1

Benefits of Helping Others

1. Improved Mental and Physical Health

Helping others can have a positive impact on both your mental and physical health. Studies have shown that those who engage in acts of kindness and altruism have lower blood pressure, increased endorphin levels, and improved psychological well-being.

2. Increased Sense of Purpose

Helping others can also give us a sense of purpose and meaning in our lives. This is especially true when we help those in need, as it can provide a sense of hope and fulfillment. People who act altruistically often report feeling a stronger connection to their community and a greater sense of satisfaction in life.

3. Improved Relationships

Helping others can also help to strengthen relationships, both those we help and those who witness our acts of kindness. This can lead to an increased sense of belonging and purpose in our lives.

4. Increased Self-Confidence

Helping others can build our self-confidence and self-esteem. We can feel a sense of accomplishment and pride by assisting those in need.

5. Increased Happiness

Finally, helping others can make us happier in the long run. We are seeing the positive effects of our actions can be a great source of motivation and satisfaction. Increased Happiness: Studies have found that people who engage in acts of kindness and generosity are generally happier than those who don't. Doing good for others can be an incredibly rewarding experience and can help lift your mood.

6. Helping others make you a bigger person

And help you to understand the importance of working together in a community and society. You will find that when you help those in need, you learn more about yourself and the world around you.

Chapter 2

The Value of Compassion

Aristotle said, "The greatest virtues are those of compassion." Compassion is a valuable virtue because it allows us to empathize with those who are suffering and to act in a way that helps them. Compassion can be expressed in many ways, from offering kind words and gestures of support to donating time or money to charitable causes. Compassion helps us to recognize the humanity and suffering of others, even when we may not fully understand their circumstances. Compassion helps us to show love and kindness, even in difficult situations. By showing compassion, we can build bridges of understanding and trust between people, helping to create a more peaceful world.

Compassion can also be seen as a form of self-care. Studies have shown that expressing compassion towards others can help reduce stress and promote feelings of connection and well-being. Practicing compassion helps to strengthen our sense of self-worth, while also making us more aware of the needs of others.

Compassion is an important part of our society and culture, and we must cultivate it in ourselves and others. Compassion can help us to make better decisions, build stronger relationships, and have a more positive outlook on life. When we make an effort to show compassion, we can create a more compassionate and caring world.

Compassion is a valuable virtue that can have far-reaching and positive effects on our lives and the lives of those around us. It can help us to be more understanding and accepting of others and to take action to help those in need. By expressing compassion, we can create a more peaceful and caring world.

It is important to remember that compassion is not just about giving to others, but also about taking care of ourselves. Practicing compassion can help us to lead more fulfilling and meaningful lives.

The Bible said, "Be kind and compassionate to one another, forgiving each other, just as in Christ God forgave you." Compassion is a valuable virtue that reminds us to show love and kindness to those around us. It helps to build bridges of understanding and trust, while also promoting our well-being. We can all benefit from learning to practice compassion in our daily lives.

Chapter 3

10 Ways to Help Others and Make a Difference in Their Lives

Helping other people ought to be a characteristic expansion of each and every business chief's liabilities. Tragically, it doesn't come as simple as you would naturally suspect. As pioneers, we frequently get too up to speed in activities or our own concerns to give individuals the assistance they with requiring. Nonetheless, somewhat recently, I've understood that the majority of my best clients, accomplices, and connections have come from me helping somebody. The following are 10 contemplations that can remind you to help other people.

1.Sharing information

One of the most straightforward ways of helping other people is to share your insight just. You don't need to be before a homeroom to educate. Each day there is a valuable chance to instruct somebody about your subject matter. The key is to continue to instruct yourself so you can remain on the ball.

2. Figuring out what's important to them

The main rule of aiding individuals ought to be to figure out what's really significant to somebody. You might invest energy and exertion assisting somebody with something that they didn't actually need assistance with. Really try to ask them where they need assistance, and remember that whenever you see an open door.

3. Sharing your assets

Contemplate the assets you've put resources into and be aware of whether they can help another person. Perhaps an engineer in your group has some additional time and one of your contacts required some assistance on a fast work. Or on the other hand, perhaps you have Cardinals season tickets and there's a game that you will not have the option to join. Hold those under-or unused assets in your subconscience and attempt to associate them with individuals who can utilize them.

4. Making them mindful of an open door

It means a lot to look out for open doors. It very well may be great press, a likely accomplice, or an overall business opportunity. When you see an open door, contemplate who could profit from being familiar with it. One of the manners in which I like to help my representatives is to help their companions, family members, or life partners on the off chance that they're searching for a task. A lot of times I can utilize my business associations with a view as a possible solid match.

5. Giving them straightforward input

Straightforward input can be extreme since certain individuals don't take productive analysis well. There is a distinction between letting somebody know that they suck and giving them genuine instances of how they can get to the next level. Certain individuals won't take it well however, over the long haul, you will assist individuals that you with needing to work with and work on the proficiency and progress of your organization also.

6. Being a brand advocate

I was at a meeting a few days ago talking with somebody from American Carriers, a client of our own. She was continuing forever about how she adored her Alter watch. She really needed to help the organization since she adored the item and needed to see them succeed. Contemplate the items and administrations that you love, and don't be bashful about telling individuals about them.

7. Giving presentations

There's a ton of lofty work out there. Somebody knows someone who is an incredible contact or client, however, they never really make the presentation. As opposed to making and breaking guarantees, try to convey a few introductions every week in fact. Be that as it may, don't allow your validity to endure a shot: ensure the individuals you're supporting are genuine.

8. Chipping in your time

Time is important and a great many people figure out that. At the point when you remove time from your day to assist a companion, they with remembering it.

I attempt and do a visitor online class every two or three weeks for contacts so they realize I'm willing to remove time from my day to impart my experience to the local area. Regardless of whether it's not something as open as an online class or web recording, put away an opportunity to help a contact. It very well may be essentially as straightforward as assisting them with moving to another home.

9. Remembering them

There are different ways of giving somebody acknowledgment. You can remember them for an article that you've composed or notice them in a discourse or show. A simple method for remembering somebody is to name them for the honor. There are incalculable honors out there that could truly assist your organization. It will be a legitimately big deal to the candidate that you considered them and needed to remember them. On a more limited size, you can include inner acknowledgment inside your organization. We have an honor called "the belt" that seems to be a WWF belt. Every week the ongoing champ picks the following victor. It's a simple method for helping a representative have a positive outlook on the strong work they've accomplished for your organization.

10. Giving gifts

Gifts can be interesting on the grounds that you would rather not "buy" people groups' approval. You need to get them a gift that seems OK and will help them. At the point when Storm Sandy hit, we sent care bundles with things that survivors could use as they recuperated from the destruction. Individuals will generally recall who assisted them when they were in with required, so putting forth an additional attempt during these times is significant.

Chapter 4

10 Ways to make a profit by helping other people

1. Start a Consulting Business

You can help businesses and individuals by providing expert advice in your field. By becoming a consultant you can help people find solutions to their challenges and make a profit.

2. Become a Freelancer

You can offer your skills and services to businesses and individuals needing help. There are many freelancing websites where you can find gigs and make money.

3. Create a Coaching Business

You can help people become better at something by becoming a coach. You can teach others how to do something such as playing a musical instrument, public speaking, cooking, or any number of skills.

4. Start a Tutoring Business

You can help people learn by offering tutoring services. You can offer tutoring services to students of all ages and help them improve their skills.

5. Become an Online Mentor

You can help people by becoming an online mentor. You can offer advice and guidance to people who need help navigating the world of business, relationships, and life in general.

6. Offer Your Services on TaskRabbit

TaskRabbit is a website that allows people to offer their services in exchange for money. You can list your skills and services on the platform and people can hire you to help them with a variety of tasks.

7. Become an Airbnb Host

You can make money by helping people find a place to stay. You can list your property on Airbnb and make money by hosting people from all over the world.

8. Start a Virtual Assistant Business

You can help busy individuals and businesses by becoming a virtual assistant. You can offer services such as scheduling appointments, organizing files, etc.

9. Become a Social Media Manager

You can help businesses and individuals grow their presence on social media. You can offer your services as a social media manager and help them reach their goals.

10. Become an Online Personal Trainer

You can help people reach their fitness goals by becoming an online personal trainer. You can offer online training programs, nutrition advice, and more.

Chapter 5

How Facebook Makes Money by helping businesses

Facebook makes money by helping businesses reach their target customers through advertising. Businesses can use the platform to create ads, target specific audiences, and measure their performance. Additionally, businesses can use Facebook's tools and services such as Facebook Pages, Facebook Ads Manager, and Facebook Audience Insights to manage their presence and campaigns on the platform. Finally, Facebook also offers services such as Facebook Live, which allow businesses to engage with customers through live streaming.

In addition to advertising, Facebook also makes money from the revenue it generates from its other products and services, such as its Marketplace, Instagram, and Oculus. Facebook also earns revenue through its payment processing services, such as Facebook Pay, and its virtual currency, Facebook Credits.

Overall, Facebook is a powerful tool for businesses to reach their target audiences and generate revenue.

As Facebook continues to evolve, so too will its monetization strategies. In 2022, Facebook is likely to continue leveraging its advertising capabilities, while also potentially introducing new revenue streams. For example, Facebook could introduce additional commerce features, such as a marketplace or shopping cart, or develop new ways to monetize its video content. Additionally, Facebook could also expand its virtual currency and payment processing services to further grow its revenue. Finally, Facebook could also explore new opportunities to monetize its artificial intelligence capabilities or data.

No matter what, Facebook will remain an important asset for businesses looking to reach their target customers and generate revenue.

With over 2 billion monthly users, Facebook's platform allows businesses to reach massive audiences and build relationships with their customers.

So, by leveraging the platform's advertising capabilities and other services, businesses can reach their target customers, generate leads, and drive sales. Ultimately, this helps businesses increase their revenue and grow their customer base.

And that's how Facebook Make Money by helping people and businesses.

Conclusion

In conclusion, helping others can have many positive effects on both the individual and the wider community. It can help to boost self-esteem, improve relationships, and create a more compassionate and understanding society. It can also help to address various environmental issues, creating a healthier and more sustainable world.

www.ingramcontent.com/pod-product-compliance
Lightning Source LLC
Chambersburg PA
CBHW050330220526
45465CB00005B/2207